A twelve week cookbook

The Cookin' Yogi's More Energy, Less Waist

Is a step by step guide to improving your diet and meal plans using whole foods. Already a healthy eater, this will help answer the question, "What's for dinner?"

FOOD FOR THOUGHT: An old Cherokee told his grandson, "My son, there is a battle between two wolves inside us all. One is Evil. It is anger, jealousy, greed, resentment, inferiority, lies & ego. The other is Good. It is joy, peace, love, hope, humility, kindness, empathy, & truth." The boy thought about… it, and asked, "Grandfather, which wolf wins?" The old man quietly replied, "The one you feed."

Sherri Mraz

Five Golden Rules to Eat By

1. Begin your meal with thanks

2. On a scale of 1 to 10, eat to a 7,
   not to full, not hungry

3. Eat in a calm environment

4. Chew your food and eat slowly

5. Watch your portion sizes

~e✺~

The Cookin' Yogi's More Energy, Less Waist
is dedicated to my family who I love so much,
my friends for always seeing the best in me,
my clients and students who taught me the
art of listening and being a good mentor, and
mostly to God who leads me in everything I
do and say.

God bless you and your journey,
Sherri

Special thanks to Lisa Magoulas for helping
me name this book.

~e✺~

Introduction

I originally started this cookbook as a twelve week group program designed to improve one's health and energy levels. Over the course of a year and many clients later, it developed into a cookbook.

This cookbook is a perfect accompaniment to my individual counseling and six week group program but can easily be used on its own as well.

It has been medically proven, (although, ironically, the medical society does not focus on this), that you will vastly improve your health if you improve your diet. I will give you information to create a holistic dietary plan. This is a whole food plan, the way God intended it. I recommend a vegetarian or flexitarian diet; which is primarily vegetarian with the occasional meat. Look at this as an adventure in the kitchen, experiment, and make it fun.

To use this book effectively I suggest that you look over the menu for the week and decide which recipes you will make. It is designed to give you five nights of healthy dinners. I know there are seven days in a week but this will give you the flexibility of not having to cook every night, although that is ideal. After you have decided which recipes you will make, you should look over your shopping list, make a copy and circle the items that you need to buy. Double check your kitchen inventory before you head out to the store. You do not need to be buying duplicates.

You can print out additional shopping lists at www.moreenergylesswaist.com

It is important to eat organic as much as possible. I hear complaints all the time that it is too expensive, but it doesn't have to be more costly. You just need to plan your meals and weekly menus in advance, this saves you money and time.

The reason I recommend organic is that it only has natural fertilizers and natural means to ward of pests. You can tell the difference by the UPC code. Organic always starts with a 9 and has 5 digits. Most of the conventional codes are only four digits and usually start with a four. Organic is much higher in phytonutrients and has a much better taste, besides who wants to eat pesticides.

Some of the recipes in this book may be new to you but some of them may be old time favorites. We will be swapping out ingredients. No more white flour, white sugar or table salt. These foods wreak havoc on your blood sugar and blood pressure, not to mention your waist line. We will replace them with whole grain flours, brown rice flour or spelt, there are other options but these are the most popular. Some sugar options are stevia, raw sugar, coconut sugar, dates, maple syrup, honey or agave nectar and your salt should be sea salt or Himalayan.

If you find one of the recipes on a given night is not something you like swap it out. In time you will build a repertoire of your favorites that you use over and over.

I love watching cooking shows. The problem is if you ate those recipes regularly you would either be heavy, unhealthy or worse yet, both. In my cooking classes I teach how to cook to improve or maintain good health.

I think people like recipes because they are guides. It takes the confusion out of guessing different taste profiles. Health coaches, take the guess work out of healthy living, and help you create a plan. Sometimes people don't even realize something isn't working until we have a health struggle.

If you could follow a recipe for a healthy life, what would it look like?

<u>Recipe for Life</u>

<u>Ingredients</u>

- 6 days Exercise
- 6 days of Eating clean (80/20 rule)
- 7 days water at least 64 oz. per day
- 8 days (hehe) Pray and/or meditate
- Keep a social balance and spend time with those you love
- Most days Love your work
- Cook with love
- Let yourself rest before moving on

<u>Directions</u>

   1. Start each day with a full glass of room temperature water.
     Add as needed throughout the day, 64 oz. is best.
   2. 30 minutes exercise daily.
   3. Keep your food as simple as you can, eat food that is close to the ground.
That means it is mostly plant based, not food that fell on the floor, haha.
   4. Find meaning in your work, we are a community, all jobs are important!
We are all important, find joy in what you do. If you can't find joy in your
work begin a plan to change it.
   5. Learn to say no, you can't do everything.
   6. Look for support. Ask for help. Do not go it alone. Build a support team.
   7. Test yourself for doneness. You will know when you do not crumble to
the slightest touch. You will feel firm but soft in the heart center.
   8. Let yourself rest when needed and get eight hours of sleep.

Life is a journey, if you are not doing all the above things don't judge yourself
but don't give up either. **One day at a time, making choices that support a
healthier body, mind and spirit.** If you fall prey to old habits that don't
support your new lifestyle, shake it off and start again, one day at a time.

I think the word to describe it is perseverance. Sometimes our biggest
breakthrough is just around the corner. Don't stop believing in yourself and your
worth.

Happy Cookin' and blessings, Sherri

My mission is to teach people how to prepare and eat high quality food. I want to see families eating together again, and not out of a box. Appreciate food, love, life and each other. It is not just what we eat that counts but what we surround ourselves with and how we think as well.

Week nine
Dinner Menu Suggestions, Pg. 72
Breakfast recipe;
Ezekiel French toast, **Pg. 72**
Shopping List, Pg. 73
Homemade Turkey Soup, Pg. 75
Coconut Curry Chicken and Green Beans, Pg. 76
Chick Pea Salad, Pg. 77
Fragrant Flavored Rice, Pg. 78
Orange ginger sauce with chicken or fish, Pg. 79

Week ten
Dinner Menu Suggestions, pg. 80
Shopping List, Pg. 81
Falafel with Dill Dressing, Pg. 82
Egg Enchiladas, Pg. 83
Easy Mac and Cheese, Pg. 84
Roasted asparagus with lemon, Pg. 84
Wasabi mashed potatoes, Pg. 85
Orange Halibut, Pg. 85

Dinner Menu Suggestions - Week one

Monday
Burger served on Ezekiel bun (either Veggie, turkey, beef)
Sweet Potato Fries & Kale Chips

Tuesday
Greek Salad with toasted pita chips

Wednesday
Buffalo tofu or chicken Brown, with rice and
Sautéed kale

Thursday
Taco Salad and Spanish rice

Friday
Pasta with Marinara and Salad

Buy organic produce and vegetables as much as you can making sure it is
fresh, not limp or old (they loose vitamins as they age)
When buying meats, make it free range, antibiotic and hormone free, raised
humanely
Ezekiel bread and rolls are usually in the freezer section

Breakfast suggestions (choose from)
> Granola cereal with fruit on top
> A couple pieces of Ezekiel toast with peanut butter
> Oatmeal or brown rice with maple syrup on it
> Eggs and toast

Every morning, first thing before your feet even hit the floor,
drink a glass of room temperature water.

Grocery Shopping List - Week One

Sweet potatoes
Amy's Veggie Burgers, or
Organic turkey or beef
Ezekiel buns
2 bunches of kale
Lettuce (preferably not iceberg)
Stuffed Grape leaves
Tomatoes
Onions
Organic feta cheese Pita's
Avocados
Fresh cilantro
Kalamata or black olives
Sliced black olives
Extra firm tofu or Chicken cutlet strips
Franks Red Hot sauce
Bag of brown rice
Corn (frozen or on ear)
Can of red or black beans
Shredded Monterey jack cheese
Salsa
Greek yogurt plain
Blue corn chips
Lime

Tomato paste
Chili powder
Brown rice pasta, whole wheat or quinoa pasta
Can of organic chopped or diced tomatoes
Garlic
Olive oil
Raw almonds
Raw walnuts
Berries
Bananas
Fruit
Eggs
Ezekiel bread
Organic milk, rice milk or almond milk
Granola
Green tea
Peanut or almond butter
Ghee
Cinnamon
Raw apple cider vinegar

Simple Starter Recipes - Week one

Baked Sweet Potato French Fries

5 sweet potatoes
1/8 cup olive oil
Pinch of salt

1. Preheat your oven to 400 degrees.
2. Wash and then cut the potatoes to look like French fries.
3. In a large baking pan, combine the sweet potatoes with the oil and salt.
4. Bake for 35 to 40 minutes until brown and crispy
*Adjust recipe to less potatoes and oil if small crowd
Can season with cayenne, Old Bay, or any variety of spices

Kale Chips

All you need is kale, olive oil, and salt, but you can add other flavorings if you like. The picture is dinosaur kale which has nutritional yeast sprinkled onto it.
Wash and dry the kale well, rub lightly with olive oil, can break into smaller pieces, place on baking sheet, sprinkle with sea salt
Bake at 350 for 15 minutes
*keep an eye on them, they can burn easily

Greek Salad

Lettuce
Tomatoes
Feta cheese
Sprinkle with kelp for iodine (helps regulate the thyroid) check with physician if on medication)
Onion
Kalamata or black olives (optional)
Olive oil with raw apple cider vinegar for dressing Toss and top with stuffed grape leaves
Serve with toasted pita's if desired

This is also my favorite go to lunch! I make it in a pretty large bowl and just sprinkle with olive oil and vinegar to taste. You can use lemon juice instead of vinegar if you like. Top it with a little kelp and enjoy. It may end up being your favorite go to lunch as well.

Buffalo Tofu

Extra Firm Tofu, or chicken strips
Grape seed or extra virgin olive oil
1/4 cup Franks Hot Sauce
2 Tbsps organic butter

Drain extra firm tofu, wrap in dish towel to absorb water
Heat skillet with 2 tbsp of grape seed or olive oil
Slice entire block of tofu into 1⁄2 inch thick pieces by 1 inch wide
Place in hot skillet
Do not touch until one side firms up then flip, or it will fall apart on you.
Once browned on outside add hot sauce, with melted butter.
Serve with brown rice, kale and extra sauce if desired,

Simple Sautéed Kale

Heat 2 tbsp extra virgin olive oil in skillet, sauté 2 crushed garlic cloves, add
entire bunch of chopped kale 1⁄4 cup water, cover and simmer 2-3 minutes

Taco Salad

Lettuce
1/4 cup Fresh cilantro
1/2 Avocado
1/4 cup corn
Black olives
Black beans or kidney beans
Greek yogurt
Monterey Jack or cheddar cheese
Organic corn chips
Lime
extra virgin olive oil and salsa of your liking

1. Make salad with lettuce; add chopped fresh cilantro, chunks of avocado
2. Add defrosted corn or slice off cob, add sliced black olives, a can of black or red beans
3. Grate cheese over top
4. Mix with little olive oil, squeeze one whole lime, dash of sea salt
*Serve with spanish rice, and corn chips, top with salsa and plain Greek yogurt

Spanish Rice

2 cups cooked brown rice
1 small onion
1 garlic clove
extra virgin olive oil
1 Tbsp tomato paste
1 Tbsp chili powder
1/4 cup water
Himalayan or sea salt

1. Sauté minced onion and one large clove minced garlic in olive oil
2. Add tomato paste and chili powder
3. Add cooked rice and 1/4 cup water. Let simmer about 5 minutes.
Salt to taste.

This recipe is great with leftover rice. When reheating rice
add a little water to moisten about a 1/4 cup. Then continue with
recipe above.

*If making rice from dry allow 45 minutes. to cook
Serve along with Taco salad

Marinara Sauce

This is a super quick sauce, it's so easy you will never buy jarred again
Ingredients
Can whole, crushed or diced organic tomatoes
garlic
Extra virgin olive oil
sea salt
red pepper flakes, pinch
dried parsley
Pasta

1. Sauté 3-4 cloves garlic in extra virgin olive oil, about 2 tbsp.
2. Add dried parsley, dash of sea salt, dash red hot pepper flakes if you like
3. Add can organic crushed tomatoes or diced if you want it chunky. I actually use whole canned tomatoes and crush them through my hand before I drop them into the pot. Let bubble a minute then turn to low
4. Boil your pasta; the sauce will be done at the same time.
5. Grate a good parmesan or Romano cheese on top

I use brown rice pasta, or the artichoke flour pasta "DeBoles" brand, You can use whole wheat or quinoa pasta, experiment to find what you like.

Cook your brown rice on the weekends if you are short of time, then use all week long, It also makes a great breakfast cereal.
Don't be afraid to use your comfort food recipes, just clean them up.
Be mindful to begin your breakup with white...
No more white flour, white sugar, white bread...only cauliflower and potatoes.

Dinner Menu Suggestions – Week Two

Monday
Spaghetti Squash with Salmon and salad

Tuesday
Black beans/rice
Salad

Wednesday
Vegetable soup
Feta green salad

Thursday
Eggplant quinoa roast
Sautéed kale (recipe found in week one)

Friday
Pasta with clam sauce
Salad

Lunch suggestions (choose from)
Bake a few sweet potatoes or yams on the weekend and store in the fridge, in a skillet melt a couple Tbsp of butter, slice yam down the middle place inner down in butter and smash to heat up, may even add a little cinnamon and sugar if having a sweet craving.
Big salad with a protein, cheese, beans, chicken or a can of tuna on top
  Sardines on crackers with salad Soup and salad
Most of the ingredients can be found in a supermarket but you will have to venture into the health food store to find certain items.

Grocery Shopping List – Week Two

Sweet potatoes
Organic salad greens
Tomatoes
Red onions
Onions
Organic spinach
Ginger root
Pineapple
Garlic
Cilantro
Organic celery
Carrots
Dried cranberries
Eggplant
Lemons
Organic red bell peppers
2 zucchini
Parsley
Bananas
Spaghetti squash
Avocado
Organic feta cheese
Salmon or Extra firm tofu
Bag of brown rice
Quinoa
Can of organic crushed or diced tomatoes
Can of chopped clams

Brown rice pasta, whole wheat, spelt or quinoa pasta or DeBoles
Chicken or vegetable broth
Dried black beans or canned
Kombu (dried seaweed)
Canellini beans canned
Small can mandarin oranges
Sliced almonds Raw almonds Raw walnuts
Eggs
Ezekiel bread
Organic milk, rice or almond milk
Organic butter
Granola
Green tea
Peanut or almond butter
Ghee or organic butter
Bag of frozen vegetables
Salsa
Extra virgin olive oil (unrefined) Raw apple cider vinegar Balsamic vinegar
Sesame oil
Tamari
Bay leaves
Kelp flakes in shaker (optional)
Cinnamon
Coriander
Oregano

Recipes - Week two

Start out your week by having your rice and beans soaked. Precook rice, beans and spaghetti squash if pressed for time to prep dinner.

<u>Baked Spaghetti Squash</u>

1. Preheat your oven to 375 degrees.
2. Cut side down in pan in 1⁄2" water.
3. Bake for 45-60 minutes until soft through the center
4. Turn over add pat of butter, salt, maple syrup or brown sugar

<u>Salmon</u>

2 Tbsps extra virgin olive oil Salmon
1/4 cup tamari
1 small red onion chopped
1 inch piece ginger root minced
1 lemon juiced
1/4 cup fresh cilantro chopped
1 cup fresh pineapple or 1 can

In a cast iron skillet or heavy bottom pan, heat pan with extra virgin olive oil, add fish, let sear a minute then begin adding in order: tamari, chopped red onion, minced fresh ginger, juice of one lemon, fresh chopped cilantro and a little chopped fresh or canned pineapple. This only takes about 15 minutes to prepare

*If cooking squash from scratch, take a half hour walk when you put squash in oven.

Black Beans and Rice

1 pound dry black beans
2 tablespoons extra virgin olive oil
1 medium onion, cut into small chunks 4 cloves garlic
1 medium bunch fresh cilantro
3 inch strip kombu
2 bay leaves
Greek Yogurt, avocado, tomato (optional)
Brown rice
*Garnish with your choices of tomato, onion, cilantro, avocado, cheese, plain Greek yogurt

1. Cover beans in water and soak for 1 to 2 hours, or overnight then drain.
2. Sauté chopped onion and garlic in extra virgin olive oil.
3. Add rinsed soaked beans, bay leaf and kombu in pan and add water to fully cover. Bring to a boil, let boil 10 minutes uncovered to let gas out, then cover and cook on medium low heat until beans are tender, 1 to 1 1/2 hours.
4. When fully cooked, add chopped cilantro and season to taste, adding in sea salt. Serve with brown rice.

Vegetable (leftover) Soup

Sauté onions, carrots, celery, garlic, 1 tsp coriander, 1 tsp oregano in extra virgin olive oil
Cover with quart of chicken or vegetable broth

Simmer about 20 minutes
Add any left over beans and rice from night before
Can add 1/4 cup of salsa
Garnish with chopped cilantro, chopped avocado and crumbled corn chips

*take 1/2 hour walk while soup is simmering

There are no measurements on your produce here because soup can be your catch all. No time to cook those vegetables you bought earlier in the week, chop them up and add them to your soup. Be creative, don't waste food. You may find you just created your favorite go to soup.

Feta Green Salad

8 cups baby spinach leaves and/or mesculin greens
1/4 medium red onion
1 tomato coarse chopped
1 1/2 cups dried cranberries
1 cup sliced almonds
1 cup crumbled feta cheese
1 small can mandarin oranges
Balsamic vinegar
Extra virgin olive oil

Place servings of spinach onto salad plates. Top with red onion, mandarin oranges, cranberries, sliced almonds and feta cheese in that order. Drizzle oil and vinegar over each salad

Eggplant-Quinoa Roast

This high-energy vegetable-rich dish needs only a green salad to complement it, and or prepare sautéed kale if desired

4 tablespoons sesame oil
1 eggplant cut into thin slices
2 Tbsp tamari
1/4 cup lemon juice
1/2 cup water
1 teaspoon grated fresh gingerroot
1 cup quinoa, rinsed
1 red bell pepper, seeded, and sliced
2 zucchini, coarsely grated
Parsley sprigs, to garnish

1. Heat the oven to 350 degrees. Heat the sesame oil in a skillet and cook the eggplant slices until golden brown. Combine the tamari, lemon juice, water, and ginger and pour over the eggplant slices reserving half of this liquid. Continue to cook for 10 minutes longer, turning once or twice, until most of the liquid is absorbed. Layer the eggplant into a baking dish overlapping slightly.
2. Add the red bell pepper and zucchini to the sesame oil remaining in the skillet and sauté until soft.
3. Cook quinoa in water for 15 mins then stir in peppers and zucchini, and spoon over the eggplant. Press down well and drizzle with remaining liquid. Return to the oven and bake for approximately 15 minutes. Serve hot, garnish with parsley sprigs.

*tip: to eliminate any bitterness from the eggplant, place slices layered between paper towels on a plate, lightly salt each layer with sea salt. Place another plate on top with a heavy object on it and let sit to press out the water before cooking.

Pasta with clam sauce

1 lb pasta
3-4 cloves garlic
extra virgin olive oil
1 Tbsp dried parsley
Sea salt
Red hot pepper flakes
1 can diced clams
1 can organic tomatoes (optional)

This is another super quick sauce
1. Start cooking your pasta.
2. In a separate pot, sauté 3-4 cloves garlic in olive oil, about 4 tbsp.
3. Add dried parsley, dash of sea salt, dash red hot pepper flakes if you like.
4. Add juice from a can of clams to sautéed garlic, reserving the clam chunks. For white sauce use a little liquid from the pasta water, if you want red sauce add a can of organic crushed tomatoes or diced if you want it chunky.
Let bubble a minute then turn to low

Important -Add clams towards the end of cooking
Cheese on this is personal preference, if wanted, grate a good parmesan or Romano cheese on top.

Remember to stay away from white flour.
If you are going gluten free use Brown rice or quinoa pasta

Dinner Menu Suggestions - Week three

Monday
Acorn Squash & Carrot Soup Salad

Tuesday
Lentils and Greens Salad

Wednesday
Salmon/Spinach Cakes
Sweet Potato fries or rice (recipe found in week one)
Sautéed kale or salad (week one)

Thursday
Glazed tofu
Brown rice
Steamed broccoli or green beans

Friday
Spicy chicken soup Salad

Food for Thought:
Watch your thoughts, they become words.
Watch your words, they become actions.
Watch your actions, they become habits.
Watch your habits, they become your character.
Watch your character, it becomes your destiny.
–Frank Outlaw

Grocery Shopping List - Week three

Sweet potatoes
Kale
Brown Rice
Acorn squash
Organic salad greens Tomatoes
Onions
Organic spinach or frozen
Beet greens or swish chard
Ginger root
Leeks
Garlic
Cilantro
Organic celery
Extra large bag of carrots
Lemons
Parsley
Bananas
Avocado
Extra firm tofu
Dark brown sugar
15 oz. can of salmon (wild)
Panko
Red or brown miso paste
Vegetable, chicken broth or bouillon (no msg)
Green or brown lentils
Raw almonds
Raw walnuts

Eggs
Ezekiel bread
Organic milk, rice or almond milk
Organic butter
Granola
Green tea
Peanut or almond butter
Ghee
Freshly grated parmesan cheese
Frozen corn
Salsa
Corn chips or taco shells

Extra virgin olive oil (unrefined)
Tamari, soy sauce or Bragg's liquid
Molasses, unsulphered
Peanut oil or dark sesame oil
Coriander
Thyme
Ground black pepper
Red pepper chili flakes
Chili powder
Cumin
Cinnamon
Oregano Cayenne pepper

All root vegetables have a necessary grounding, soothing effect on the body and mind. Root vegetables also naturally satisfy the cravings for sweets that many of us experience. Rather than depending on processed sugar, add corn, carrots, onions, beets, winter squashes, sweet potatoes, and yams to your diet. The longer they cook, the sweeter they get.

Other vegetables that cut sugar cravings may be a surprise: red radishes, daikon, green cabbage and burdock are among them. These vegetables are also known for their fat- burning qualities.

Acorn Squash & Carrot Soup

1 acorn squash, cut in chunks
1 pound organic carrots, cut in chunks
1 medium onion, chopped
2 inch piece of fresh ginger
6 tbs. unsalted organic butter
3 tbs. dark brown sugar
5 cups broth, or water with organic vegetable powder added to taste (3 or 4 tbs)
Dash cayenne pepper Salt to taste
Fresh parsley and/or cilantro

1. Place first group of ingredients in slow cooker. Set to low heat and cook all day, or place in a heavy-bottomed stock pot and simmer until soft, at least 30 minutes.
2. When cooking is completed, puree all ingredients together with an immersion blender, regular blender or food processor. If using a regular blender or food processor, puree in small batches, then combine.
3. Blend in cayenne pepper and salt to taste.
*Serve warm garnished with chopped parsley and/or cilantro.

Lentils and Greens

1 cup green or brown lentils, rinsed
2 cups vegetable broth
1 bunch beet greens or swiss chard
1 teaspoon red or brown miso paste to impart salty/smokey flavor
black pepper
extra virgin olive oil
small onion
2 cloves garlic
Saute onion and garlic in olive oil

1. Add rinsed lentils and vegetable broth, cook until desired tenderness and most of liquid is absorbed.
2. Clean, chop and lightly steam greens.
3. Combine lentils, greens, miso, drizzle of extra virgin olive oil, salt and black pepper to taste.
Garnish with chopped cilantro

* When shopping, stick to the perimeter of the store as much as possible, this is where the fresh food is. The processed food is in the inner isles.

Alaska Canned Salmon Spinach Cakes

1 package frozen spinach or 1 pound fresh
1 15 oz. can Alaska Red Salmon, drained (wild caught)
1 1/2 cups panko
1/2 cup finely chopped onion
3 large eggs
2 Tbsp extra virgin olive oil
1/4 cup grated parmesan
1 tsp soy or tamari
1 tsp coriander
1 or 2 cloves minced garlic
1/4 tsp dried thyme
dash black pepper
1/4 chopped walnuts
Optional - Greek yogurt, dried dill, lemon, sea salt

1. Preheat oven to 350, grease baking sheet
2. Steam spinach and drain
3. In large mixing bowl, combine spinach with remaining ingredients, mix thoroughly and form into balls
4. Place balls 1 " apart on baking sheet, flatten and bake for 30 minutes

Optional dill dressing:
1/2 Greek yogurt, 1 Tbsp dried dill, 1/2 tsp sea salt and 1 Tbsp lemon juice

34

Glazed Tofu

1 carton extra firm tofu
2 lg. garlic cloves, minced
2 tbs. fresh lemon or lime juice
1⁄2 cup soy sauce
1 tbs. molasses
2 tsp roasted peanut or dark
sesame oil
2 tbs. chopped cilantro
Freshly ground pepper
1 or 2 tbs olive oil
1 tsp Grated ginger

Drain the tofu by wrapping in a
dish towel and blotting well.
While tofu is draining combine all
other ingredients together in a
food processor

Heat a large cast-iron or regular
skillet and coat bottom with a little
oil

Once hot add the tofu slices,
about 1⁄2 in thick is best by 1"
(too thin is difficult to turn)

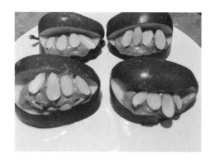

Apple Lips and Teeth

Funny treat to make with the kids;
cut apples into v shapes, add a nut
butter and almond slices.

Brown until golden then turn over
slowly add the marinade and
cook down until syrupy, reserving
some marinade for later use.

*Serve with brown rice and
steamed broccoli or green beans
You can use this glaze recipe
with chicken, fish or shrimp. I also
use it over veggies, amazing!

Spicy Soup with Avocado

This was my original signature soup. It is so delicious with it's spicy lemony taste. I especially love fresh chopped avocado on top with a sprinkling of crushed corn chips and another squeeze of lemon. You can easily add left over shredded chicken and turn it into a chicken soup.

1 tsp olive oil
1 cup chopped leeks or onions
3 stalks of celery sliced
3 or 4 carrots sliced
1 tsp black pepper
1 pinch red pepper chili flakes
1 tsp chili powder
1 tsp cumin
1 tsp coriander
1 tsp marjoram or oregano
1 cup rinsed brown rice
1 cup fresh or frozen corn
6-8 cups of chicken stock (optional to add chicken)
1/4 cup chopped cilantro
(reserve 4 large sprigs to chop and add as garnish)
1 cup avocado, cut into cubes
2 lemons
1 heaping Tbsp of salsa
Organic corn chips
If desired top with a dollop of Greek yogurt

In a pot heat oil, add onions, celery, carrots and all the spices. If mixture begins to get dry add a little of the broth. Cook for about 5 minutes. Add the remainder of the chicken broth, add the rice and cook 30 minutes. Next add the corn and the cilantro. Continue to simmer until the vegetables and rice are soft. Add the juice of 1 whole lemon squeezed and the salsa.

Ladle into bowls, spoon some avocado into the center of each bowl, sprinkle with cilantro, crumbled tortillas, another squeeze of lemon, and yogurt if desired.

Dinner Menu Suggestions – Week four

Monday
Collard Green and Black Eyed Pea Soup
Salad and corn bread

Tuesday
Asian Chicken Salad
With left over soup or organic tomato soup

Wednesday
Tacos

Thursday
Garden Soup
Salad

Friday
Shrimp with Broccoli Pasta
Salad

Try a **green smoothie** this week. Throw some kale or spinach in the blender (Vitamix is the best), add slice of fresh ginger, and fruit, with either water, coconut water, almond milk and ice. Adjust to what you like. Great way to start the day. (add ingredients to your shopping list)

Grocery Shopping List– Week four

Organic potatoes
Organic carrots
Organic celery
Organic collard greens
2 or 3 Limes
2 or 3 Lemons
Napa cabbage (use twice)
Snow peas
Cucumber
Scallions
Organic Red or yellow pepper
Cilantro
Fresh mint
Organic romaine
Tomatoes
Onions
Ginger root (store in freezer)
Garlic
Parsley
Bananas
Broccoli
Bag of sundried tomatoes
Eggs
Ezekiel bread
Brown Rice
Pasta
Granola
Green Tea
Peanut or almond butter
Ghee

Corn tortillas
Greek yogurt plain
Salsa
Organic Monterey Jack or cheddar
Organic butter
Organic milk, rice or almond milk
Freshly grated parmesan cheese
Organic feta cheese
Edamame
Corn
Bag of peeled shrimp
15 oz diced tomatoes
2 cans black eyed peas or dried
Refried beans
Canallini beans
Black olives
Artichoke hearts
2 –3 qts. Vegetable broth or bouillon
Extra virgin olive oil (unrefined)
Tamari, soy sauce or Bragg's
Hot sauce
Rice vinegar
Dark Asian sesame oil
Dijon mustard
Turmeric
Cumin
Oregano
Cayenne pepper
Red pepper chili flakes
Organic chicken breasts
corn bread

Collard Green and Black-Eyed Pea Soup

6 cups organic vegetable broth
1 onion, chopped
4 cloves of garlic, minced
15 oz canned tomatoes, chopped
1 tsp. ground turmeric (helps to reduce inflammation in the body)
1 tsp. ground cumin
1 tsp. dried oregano
Cayenne pepper to taste
2 potatoes, cubed
2 cans black-eyed peas or dried
4 carrots, chopped
2 celery stalks, chopped
1 bunch collard greens, cleaned and chopped
Salt and freshly ground pepper to taste
Louisiana hot sauce, to taste

I prefer dried beans but then they need to be soaked overnight and then cooked. It is more time consuming but worth it. If using canned check for chemicals in the ingredients, all that should be in there is beans, water, sea salt and maybe kombu. Kombu is seaweed which helps to make the beans more digestible and helps eliminate gas. You can cook the beans with it, then discard it after the beans are done or mince and leave it in for the extra omega's and vitamins.

1. In a soup pot, sauté the onion, garlic and spices for 5 minutes.
2. Add the stock and tomatoes, bring to a boil.
3. Add the potatoes, black-eyed peas, carrots, celery and collards.
4. Simmer for 30 minutes and season with hot sauce.
Serve with corn bread if desired.

ASIAN CHICKEN SALAD

For vinaigrette
1/4 cup low sodium soy or tamari sauce
2 Tbsp. rice vinegar
2 Tbsp. fresh lime juice
2 Tbsp. Olive oil
1 1/2 Tbsp. dark Asian sesame oil
1 Tbsp. Dijon mustard
1 heaping Tbsp. peeled finely grated fresh ginger
1/2 Tsp. crushed red pepper

For salad
4 cups coarsely shredded cooked chicken (about 1 1/2 lbs.)
1/2 lb. Napa cabbage, coarsely shredded (3 1/2cups)
1/4 lb. snow peas cut diagonally into 1 inch pieces
1 cucumber, quartered lengthwise, cut into 1/2" pcs and deseeded
4 scallions, finely chopped
3 celery stalks, chopped
1 red or yellow pepper, julienned
1 1/2 cups of cooked edamame, (find in the freezer case at store)
1/2 cup each of fresh cilantro and mint

Whisk together all vinaigrette ingredients.
Toss salad ingredients with vinaigrette in a large bowl until well combined. Sprinkle with sliced almonds (optional)

Recipe courtesy of Lois Orth-Zitoli, Full Circle Health, Inc.
My first health coaching business partner and friend.

Tacos

Corn tortillas
Refried Beans
Romaine lettuce
Frozen corn or cut from cob
Sliced black olives
1 chopped tomato
1/2 small onion chopped
1/4 cup chopped cilantro
olive oil
1 lemon juiced
Monterey Jack Cheese
*Optional , Spanish rice (recipe in week 1)

Heat refried beans for the bottom layer in your taco
Make a salad of shredded romaine, corn, sliced black olives, chopped tomatoes, chopped onion, chopped cilantro tossed with small amount of olive oil and lemon.
Use corn taco shells, layer beans or meat, salad, rice (if using) top with grated organic cheese, plain Greek Yogurt
and Salsa.

*No one will know that your yogurt is not sour cream

Even though this is a cookbook, and what you eat is super important, what you surround yourself with can be even more important! We need to find ways to eliminate stress in our life.

Practice being in the moment.
Take some deep breaths.
Watching what we say, eliminate complaining, speaking positive words.
Working on forgiveness.
Practicing self love, do something nice for yourself everyday.

Garden Soup

Ingredients

1 medium onion, chopped
1 tablespoon olive oil
1 carrot, chopped
4 garlic cloves, thinly sliced
2 quarts organic low-salt vegetable broth
1 can (28 ounces) whole or diced tomatoes, undrained
1 can canellini beans
2 cups water
1 small head cabbage, thinly sliced
1/2 teaspoon hot red pepper sauce (optional)
Salt and freshly ground black pepper (optional)

Optional garnishes: chopped fresh parsley, chopped fresh cilantro

Cooking Directions

Heat a large saucepan over medium-high heat, add oil, then onion; cook 5 minutes, stirring occasionally. Stir in carrot and garlic, cook until tender. Add broth, tomatoes, water, cabbage and beans; simmer uncovered 20 minutes. Season to taste, add hot sauce, salt and pepper, if desired. Garnish with parsley or cilantro. Serve with salad and toasted Ezekiel buns.

Shrimp and Broccoli

1 lb. shrimp (peeled and deveined)
1 head broccoli
6-8 cloves garlic, chopped
5 sun dried tomatoes, sliced
Pinch crushed red pepper
1/2 cup extra virgin olive oil
3 Tbsp organic butter
1 lb. brown rice , whole wheat or guinoa pasta
Can black olives sliced
Can or jar artichoke hearts
1 cup reserved pasta water
1/4 cup Parmesan cheese
4 ozs. Feta cheese

Cut broccoli into florets, peel and slice stems.
Steam until crisp tender, about 4 mins., drain.

Cook pasta until al dente, about 4-6 mins.,
Drain , return to pot, reserving 1 cup liquid.

Heat olive oil and butter over medium heat.
Add garlic, red pepper, sundried tomatoes and
shrimp, saute for about 3 more minutes.
Add broccoli for 2 minutes, then black olives
and sliced artichokes.

Combine mixture with pasta, adding pasta
liquid as needed, and cheese.

This recipe is a little more of a splurge but it will be one of your favorite go to recipes when you have company over.

It is creamy and delicious and by changing out the pasta you don't have to go into a pasta carb shock.

See, you can still do decadent.

Dinner Menu Suggestions - Week five

Monday
Red kidney beans and rice, Sauteed Kale or Swiss Chard Salad (from wk 1)

Tuesday
Mexican bean salad

Wednesday
Vegetarian Chili Salad

Thursday
Mexican Pizza

Friday
Minestrone Vegetarian Soup Salad

The focus of the recipes this week is on Red Kidney Beans. Beans are a good source of protein which is needed in the diet to retain and rebuild muscle. It contains the amino acid tyrosine which gives the brain a boost and elevates mood. Protein also gives the body a sense of feeling satisfied from our meals.

Get over the fat phobia. Remember we need healthy fat in our diets. Foods such as avocados, nuts and seeds contain an enzyme called lipase which assists in breaking down and digesting fats. Nuts and seeds such as walnuts and sunflower seeds are full of omega 3's which keep our immune system and skin healthy.

I know this may be hard to believe but, if consuming dairy full fat is actually better for you than low fat. The chemicals to reduce the fat are worse than the fat! Always buy organic dairy whenever possible.

Grocery Shopping List - Week five

2 bags dried red kidney beans
Organic potatoes
Organic carrots
Organic celery
Organic collard greens, swiss chard, spinach or kale
Limes
Lemons
Cabbage
Organic Red or yellow pepper
Organic green pepper
Cilantro
Organic romaine or mixed salad greens
Tomatoes
Onions
Garlic
Parsley
Bananas

Eggs
Ezekiel bread
Brown Rice
Granola
Green tea
Peanut or almond butter
Ghee

Corn tortillas
Greek yogurt plain
Salsa
Organic Monterey Jack or cheddar
Organic butter
Organic milk, rice or almond milk
Frozen corn
2 28 oz cans whole tomatoes Black olives
Vegetable flavoring
Extra virgin olive oil (unrefined)
Grape seed oil
Hot sauce
Dry red wine

Turmeric
Cumin
Oregano
Cayenne pepper
Chili powder
Bay leaves
Dried basil

Week 5 (beans and protein)

Protein is necessary to help muscles recover from exercise. It contains necessary amino acids, one of which is tyrosine which gives the brain a boost and elevates mood. Also, by adding in sufficient protein you will have a feeling of being satisfied by your meals. Some good vegetarian sources of protein are lentils, chickpeas, navy beans, nuts, seeds, tofu and tempeh.

Add in complete protein combinations like rice and beans, peanut butter and whole grain bread. Tofu is a complete protein on its own, which can be added to a stir fry for a nutrient dense meal.

Red kidney Beans and Brown Rice

Ingredients
1 bag dried Kidney beans, previously rinsed, soaked and rinsed again
1 onion, chopped
4 cloves of garlic, minced
1/2 tsp. ground turmeric (helps to reduce inflammation in the body)
1 tsp. dried cilantro
Salt and freshly ground pepper to taste
In a soup pot, sauté the onion, garlic and spices for 5 minutes. Add beans and simmer for 60–90 minutes and season with salt.
Serve with brown rice, sautéed greens and a homemade corn bread
*Save some beans for the remainder of the week – Reserve 2 cups cooked beans to make refried beans, reserve 2 cups for chili, and 1/2 cup for salad add in, any remaining beans can go into the minestrone soup on Friday.
*This is an example of how to roll ingredients during the week. Sick of beans this week, freeze and use later.

Mexican Bean Salad

For salad
1/2 cup kidney beans
1/2 cup corn
Mixed salad greens
1/2 bunch chopped fresh cilantro
1/2 onion chopped
1 yellow or red pepper
2 stalks celery
Monterey Jack or Cheddar Cheese

For vinaigrette
2 Tbsp. fresh lime juice
2 Tbsp. Olive oil
Salt and pepper

Mix together in large bowl all salad ingredients.
Top with grated cheese.

Whisk together all vinaigrette ingredients.
Toss salad ingredients with vinaigrette in a large bowl until
well combined.

Vegetarian Chili

You won't miss the meat in this chili but if you must have it add a humanely raised, organic turkey or ground beef.

Ingredients

2 cups beans
1/2 cup dry red wine
2 tbsp olive oil
1 cup chopped onion
1/2 cup chopped green pepper
3 cloves garlic minced
1 can whole peeled tomatoes
1 tsp oregano
1 tbsp chili powder
1/2 tsp cumin
Salt to taste
Cayenne pepper to taste

Directions

Sauté chopped onion, garlic, and green pepper, add red wine, can of tomatoes, oregano, chili powder, cumin and beans, add a little water if needed.

Simmer 30 minutes.

Add cayenne and salt to taste,

May top with Greek yogurt and shredded cheese.

Mexican Pizza

Refried beans
2 cups beans
One onion
2 garlic cloves

Soft corn taco shells
Grape seed oil
Sliced black olives
Monterey Jack or Cheddar Cheese
*cilantro
*Plain Greek yogurt

To make refried beans – sauté one minced onion in olive oil till soft add 2 minced cloves of garlic, add beans, pinch of salt and mash with potato masher. Add a little water and cover for 10 minutes on low.

Use soft corn taco shells; heat grape seed oil in a hot cast iron skillet or griddle pan, cook shells, one at a time, on each side until crispy. Drain on paper towels. Lay shells out on a cookie sheet; spread a layer of beans, top with sliced black olives, salsa and grated Monterey Jack or cheddar cheese. Place in oven on 450 degrees till cheese is melted.
Can top with *minced cilantro and *plain Greek yogurt.

Minestrone Vegetable Soup

Ingredients
2 tbsp olive oil
1 onion, chopped
3 - 4 carrots, chopped
1 cup cubed potatoes
2-3 stalks celery
4 garlic cloves, thinly sliced
1 can (28 ounces) whole or diced tomatoes, undrained
1 cup red kidney beans (or whatever beans you have left from the week)
8 cups water
Vegetable flavoring to taste
1 cup cabbage, thinly sliced
1/2 cup fresh parsley chopped
1 bay leaf
1 tsp dried basil
1/2 teaspoon hot red pepper sauce (optional)
Salt and pepper

Cooking Directions:

Heat a large saucepan over medium high heat, add oil, then onion; cook 5 minutes, stirring occasionally. Stir in carrots, potatoes, celery and garlic, cook another five minutes. Add tomatoes, water, bouillon, cabbage, spices and beans; simmer covered 30-45 minutes.

Optional - may add 1 cup uncooked pasta for last 15 minutes. Season to taste; add hot sauce, salt and pepper, if desired.

Serve with salad and toasted Ezekiel buns

Dinner Menu Suggestions – Week six

Monday
Quinoa Vegetable Melody
Serve with steamed fish, or Glazed Tofu (recipe from week 2)
Salad

Tuesday
Tofu in Red Coconut Curry Sauce and Salad

Wednesday
Pasta Fagiola and Salad

Thursday
Italian Frittata and Salad

Friday
Leftover Vegetarian Soup and Salad

The focus of the recipes this week is again on Protein. Quinoa, tofu, cancelli beans and eggs are a good sources of protein and help the body have a sense of feeling satisfied.

Grocery Shopping List - Week Six

Organic potatoes
Organic carrots
Organic celery
spinach or kale
Lemons or Limes
2 Organic Red peppers
Cilantro
Organic romaine or mixed salad
greens
Tomatoes
Onions
Garlic
Parsley
Bananas
Ginger
Scallions
Mint
Bok Choy
Broccoli

Eggs
Ezekiel bread
Brown Rice
Granola
Green tea
Peanut or almond butter
Ghee
Organic butter

Organic milk, rice or almond milk
Extra firm tofu
2 28 oz whole tomatoes
1 can cannellini beans
Tamari
vegetable flavoring, no MSG
Extra virgin olive oil (unrefined)
Coconut or peanut oil
Can of coconut milk
Red curry paste
Can chicken broth
Tomato paste
Organic Spices (not irradiated)
Bay leaves
Dried basil
Red pepper flakes
Saffron
Grains
Quinoa
Pasta preferably brown rice

Use up fresh cilantro, mint,
parsley etc. in raw salads, don't
throw out!

Quinoa

Quinoa contains all eight amino acids to make it a complete protein, equal in content to milk. It is high in B vitamins, iron, zinc, potassium, calcium, vitamin E and magnesium. It is a pseudo grain which is actually a seed. It is not a carbohydrate and does not elevate your blood sugar; it is gluten free and easy to digest.

Quinoa is a fast cooking grain, which only needs a quick rinse prior to cooking. By rinsing you are eliminating any bitter taste from the saponin which is a naturally occurring pesticide. Place rinsed quinoa in a dry heated skillet and sauté dry. You will begin to smell a nutty aroma which adds a delicious nutty flavor. By adding in the kale which is a cruciferous vegetable, you are adding the extra antioxidants and cancer fighting properties. The addition of garlic and scallion which both come from the alliums family are also powerhouses full of antioxidants. Ginger is also an excellent antioxidant, alleviates gastrointestinal distress and has anti-inflammatory effects. The minimal cooking time maintains their phytochemical properties which help to boost the immune system. If you do not like kale choose broccoli, cauliflower, cabbage, or bok choy. These vegetables are also from the cruciferous family. Use what you have; you can add something in, leave something out, just be creative and have fun.

Quinoa and Veggie Melody

1 cup quinoa (plain or red)
1 garlic clove finely minced or pressed
2 cups water (may use vegetable or chicken broth)
1 carrot diced small
4 or 5 stalks of kale chopped (also chop leaves)
1/4 cup of chopped fresh cilantro
Juice of one lemon or lime
1-2 tbsp of tamari or Bragg's Liquid Amino Acids (a high grade soy sauce, non-GMO)
1 tbsp of fresh grated ginger
2 chopped scallions
1 small tomato (optional)
Few sprigs of fresh mint (optional)

Directions:
*Heat dry skillet on high, rinse quinoa in a small strainer, drain and then add directly to hot skillet to toast. You will begin to notice a nutty smell.
*Add garlic over the top, stir and immediately add the water or broth. Cover and simmer for 10 minutes on low heat.
*Add the carrots and the chopped kale stalks stirring and cooking with cover on for 3 minutes. Then add finely chopped kale leaves at the end and simmer for another minute or two until you reach the consistency of cooked rice (all liquid will be cooked out).
*Uncover and add the cilantro, lemon or lime juice, tamari sauce, and the scallions all at once. Serve in a bowl with chopped fresh tomato and fresh mint on top.

Tofu in Red Coconut Curry Sauce

1 package of extra firm tofu, cut into small cubes
1 tbs. coconut oil or peanut oil
3 garlic cloves minced
1 inch piece fresh ginger, minced
1 bunch scallions, including tops sliced
1 can coconut milk
2 tbs. tamari sauce
1-2 tsp. red curry paste
Red bell pepper
3-4 stalks bok choy
3-4 stalks broccoli

*In large skillet sauté red pepper and broccoli for two to three minutes add garlic, ginger, and scallions.
*Then add the bok choy and the can of coconut milk, tamari, red curry paste and tofu cut into small cubes.

Any vegetables can be substituted or left out completely. You may substitute shrimp or chicken strips for tofu.
Serve over brown rice or rice noodles

Here's a quick and easy breakfast tip

Easy Overnight Oatmeal
- 1/4 cup steel cut oats and 1 1/4 cup water
- Put in a pot, bring to a boil, cover and shut off.
- Remove from stove and leave covered till morning.
In AM, reheat, add berries, nuts, seeds, maple syrup, you pick.

Pasta Fagiola

Ingredients
1 small onion, chopped
3 cloves garlic, minced
2 teaspoons dried basil
Pinch of red pepper flakes
salt to taste
1 (14.5 ounce) can chicken broth
1 tbsp tomato paste
1 cup cooked brown rice ditalini pasta
Reserve 1/2 cup pasta water
1 (15 ounce) can canellini beans, with liquid

1. Cook pasta until al dente about 6 minutes. Drain and reserve one cup of pasta water.
2. In a large saucepan over medium heat, add onion, garlic, basil, red pepper and salt until onion is translucent. Stir in chicken broth, and tomato paste, and simmer on low for 5 - 10 minutes.

3. Add pasta and drained/rinsed beans and simmer 2-3 minutes
4. Let rest about 5 minutes, add a little of the reserved pasta water if needed.

5. Serve with grated Parmesan cheese and or minced fresh parsley sprinkled on top.

Italian Frittata

2 tbsp extra virgin olive oil
1 red bell pepper, seeded,
thinly sliced
1 cup chopped broccoli
1/2 onion chopped
1 small potato
2-3 strings saffron (optional)
6 eggs scrambled

1. In a cast iron skillet sauté potatoes in 2 Tbsp olive oil, add a little water, cover and steam potatoes till soft 5-10 minutes.
2. Add broccoli, and red pepper, cover and simmer 5 minutes.
3. Grind saffron between fingers add to mixture and pour scrambled eggs on top. Cook without stirring for 3-4 minutes or until the underside of the frittata is cooked but the top is still runny.
4. Place under hot broiler for a minute or two until top is golden.

Garnish with grated cheese and minced fresh parsley or basil.

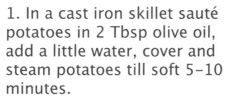

Leftover Soup

Ingredients
2 tbsp olive oil
1 onion, chopped
3 - 4 carrots, chopped
1 small potato cubed
2-3 stalks celery
3 garlic cloves, thinly sliced
1 can whole or diced
tomatoes, undrained
8 cups water
1 tsp Vogue Vegetable
flavoring
1 bay leaf
Salt and black pepper
(optional)
*Chopped leftover vegetables
and cooked grains (clean out
the fridge)

Heat a large saucepan over
medium-high heat, add
oil, then onion; cook 5
minutes, stirring occasionally.
Stir in carrots, potatoes, celery
and garlic, cook another five
minutes.
Add tomatoes, water,
bouillon, bay leaf, and leftover veggies; simmer covered
30-45 minutes.
Optional - may add left over
cooked grains for last 5
minutes,
season to taste.
Serve with salad and toasted
Ezekiel bun

Dinner Menu Suggestions – Week Seven

Monday
Coconut Adzuki Beans and Salad

Tuesday
Asparagus Soup
Toasted Ezekiel buns and Salad

Wednesday
Broccoli Rabe
Broiled fish and rice and Salad

Thursday
Quinoa with Curried Legumes and Greens and Salad

Friday
Pasta with Broccoli, Garlic and lemon and Salad

The focus of the recipes this week is on Brain Food. Quinoa, Adzuki, lentils and garbanzo beans are a good source of **protein** which contains the **amino acid L-tyrosine** which gives the brain a boost, elevates alertness and elevates mood. **Omega 3's** are vital for brain power. Fatty fish contain the most omega 3's, the highest amount is found in mackerel, followed by salmon, then halibut. Sardines are also an excellent source. Good quality oils have omega 3's as well, nuts and seeds and dark leafy greens. **Folate (folic acid)** is important for brain metabolism and necessary for prevention of birth defects in unborn babies. High concentrations can be found in bananas, lemons, leafy greens and beans.

Grocery Shopping List ~Week seven

Butternut squash
Hot pepper (optional)
2 Red onions
2 bunches asparagus
2 bunches broccoli rabe
Organic carrots
Organic celery
Organic kale or mustard greens
Beet greens or Swiss chard
Broccoli
Lemons
Organic romaine or mixed greens
Tomatoes
Onions
Garlic
Fresh parsley
Bananas

Eggs
Ezekiel bread
Brown Rice
Granola
Green tea
Peanut or almond butter
Ghee

Hard parmesan cheese
Organic butter

Organic milk, rice or almond milk

Adzuki beans
Kombu (dried seaweed)
Brown or green lentils
Cup garbanzo beans can or dried

Tamari or low sodium soy
7 cups vegetable broth or
flavoring
Extra virgin olive oil
Can of coconut milk

Sea salt
Ground nutmeg
Lemon pepper or Mrs. Dash
Curry powder
Grains
Quinoa
Pasta (brown rice, spelt, or
DeBoles brand)

Mackerel, salmon or halibut
Chicken or shrimp (optional)

Coconut Adzuki Beans

1 cup of dried adzuki beans
1 three-inch piece of kombu
1 pound of butternut squash, peeled and diced
1 can of coconut milk
1 hot pepper (optional)
2 red onions, finely diced
1 clove of garlic, minced
2 tablespoons of olive oil

1. Put the adzuki beans water and kombu in a large saucepan and bring to a boil. Simmer uncovered for 30 minutes or until beans are soft, drain liquid.
2. In a separate pot, stir fry onions, garlic, and squash for 3-5 minutes
3. Add coconut milk, the whole pepper and drained adzuki beans mixture.
4. Cover and cook on medium for 20 minutes; Remove the hot pepper and discard.

Serve over brown rice or quinoa. Add kale or mustard greens for more interest, and more vitamins!

Recipe created and donated by "Oz Kitchens"

"You are perfect, whole and complete just the way you are."

Asparagus Soup

1 1/2 pounds asparagus
trimmed & chopped
1 onion, diced
4 cups vegetable broth
1 tsp. sea salt
1/2 tsp. fresh ground nutmeg
1 Tbsp. extra virgin olive oil

1. In a large saucepan
combine asparagus, onion,
vegetable broth and cook until
vegetables are soft.
2. Add salt, nutmeg & olive
oil.
3. Puree in blender or food
processor, making sure to
only fill container 1/2 full to
prevent accidents, or use an
immersion blender.
4. Garnish with pine nuts,
minced fresh parsley,
croutons, yogurt or creme
fraiche.

Broccoli Rabe

2 bunches of broccoli rabe
4 cloves of garlic minced
1 Tblsp. of extra virgin olive oil
Freshly grated Parmigiana cheese

1. Chop off lower 1 inch from stalks
and discard. Chop the stalks and
leaves into 1 inch pieces; wash well.
2. Blanch broccoli rabe in a pot of
salted simmering water for
approximately 5 minutes. Stems
should be tender. Remove from heat
and drain (this helps to remove the
bitter taste).
3. Heat olive oil in a large skillet and
add minced garlic. Cook for about 1
minute until garlic is fragrant but not
burned.
4. Add chopped rabe and sauté for 5-
8 minutes. Taste and season with salt
and freshly ground pepper.
5. Drizzle with lemon juice and/or
sprinkle with cheese if desired.

*Serve with rice and broiled fish
seasoned with lemon pepper or Mrs.
Dash's seasoned salt and lemon juice.

Quinoa with Curried Legumes & Greens

1 1/2 cups quinoa
3 cups water or vegetable stock
Pinch of sea salt
1 tablespoon extra virgin olive oil
1 yellow onion, diced
2-3 cloves of garlic, crushed
1 large stalk of celery, diced
1 large carrot, diced
1 cup brown or green lentils
1/2 cup garbanzo beans, cooked or canned
Handful of dark leafy greens, such as beet greens or chard
1 tablespoon curry powder
Lightly salt (with sea salt or low-sodium soy sauce) and pepper, to taste

1. Wash quinoa and toast in a dry pan for a few minutes, until it smells nutty.
2. Add water (or stock) and salt to quinoa. Bring to a boil, and then turn heat to low and simmer, covered for 20 minutes.
3. While quinoa is cooking, prepare lentils.
4. Put the lentils in a small pot and cover with water to an inch above lentils. Bring to a boil and simmer for 15 minutes. Drain and reserve a small amount of cooking water.
5. Heat oil in a skillet and sauté onions and garlic for 5 minutes on medium.
6. Add celery and carrots and sauté for another 5 minutes.
7. Add garbanzo beans, cooked lentils, greens, and seasonings. Cover and cook 3-5 minutes until greens are wilted.
8. Spread cooked quinoa onto serving platter.
9. Spoon curried legumes over the top and serve.
* Make this your own by adding different vegetables, cauliflower is nice.

Pasta with Broccoli, Garlic and Lemon

Ingredients
1 pound whole grain pasta such as penne
1 medium head of broccoli
4 cloves garlic
1 lemon
2 Tsp. Extra virgin olive oil

Directions
1. Cook pasta according to directions.
2. Separate broccoli into small florets & slice garlic.
3. Briefly steam broccoli and garlic in saucepan in 2 Tsp. extra virgin olive oil.
4. Combine pasta, broccoli, garlic and coat with extra oil.
5. Sprinkle with lemon zest.

*Add chicken, shrimp, pine nuts or grated parmesan cheese if desired.

You are more than half way through! How do you feel? Are you practicing eating mindful? Time for a healthy surprise treat.

Sweet Lassi

1 pomegranate, seeded
1 cup Greek yogurt
1 cup water
2 Tbsp honey
1 lime peeled
1 cup pineapple chucks

Puree all together in blender, Vitamix works best. I add ice before blending.

Dinner Menu Suggestions ~ Week Eight

Monday
Black Bean Blast
Served with choice of grain, green and salad

Tuesday
Ginger broiled Salmon with sauteed swiss chard

Wednesday
Roasted Cauliflower with Fresh Herbs and Parmesan
Leftover black beans and rice and Salad

Thursday
Brussel sprouts with maple mustard sauce
Serve with grilled chicken, fish or tofu and Salad

Friday
Vegetable Cabbage Soup and Salad
Ezekiel bread or whole grain roll

Breakfast suggestions (choose from)
Granola cereal with fruit on top, with milk or on top of yogurt
A couple pieces of Ezekiel toast with peanut butter, raw honey or organic jelly
Oatmeal Add berries, nuts, seeds, maple syrup; whatever you like.
Lunch suggestions (choose from)
Salad with a protein, cheese, beans, chicken or a can of tuna on top
Sardines on crackers with salad
Soup and salad
Leftovers
Sweet potato

Grocery Shopping List ~ Week eight

Bell pepper
Lime
Fresh cilantro
Ginger root
Cauliflower
Organic carrots
Organic celery
Swiss chard
Lemons
Organic romaine or mixed greens
Organic tomatoes
Onions
Garlic
Bananas
Brussels sprouts
Cabbage
Fresh parsley
Eggs
Ezekiel bread
Brown Rice
Granola
Green tea
Peanut or almond butter
Ghee
Hard parmesan cheese
Organic butter
Organic milk, or almond milk

Corn
Black Beans dried or canned
Can of organic whole tomatoes
Umeboshi plum vinegar
Extra virgin olive oil
Organic coconut oil
Can of coconut milk
Vogue Vegetable powder
kombu
Cinnamon
Cumin
Sea salt or Himalayan
Cayenne pepper
Parsley
Tarragon
Thyme
Black pepper
Maple syrup
Dijon mustard

Specialty
Mackerel, salmon or halibut
White meat, fish or tofu for Thursday

Black Bean Blast

4 cups black beans, cooked
2 tablespoons cinnamon
2 teaspoons cumin
1 onion, diced
2-3 cloves garlic, minced
1 tablespoon olive oil
1 bell pepper, chopped
1 teaspoon salt
Pinch of cayenne
1 lime
1/2 cup cilantro, chopped
2" piece of Kombu (seaweed), rinsed and soaked for 10 minutes prior to use.

1. Wash and soak 2 cups of dried beans the night before, with kombu.
2. Rinse off soaking water, place into pot with 3 1/2 cups of water and bring to a boil, uncovered. Add cinnamon and cumin; cover and cook for 1 hour. (If you use canned black beans, rinse, empty into pot, mix with cinnamon and cumin. Cover and cook on medium for about 10 minutes.
3. In a pan, sauté onions and garlic with oil.
4. Mix beans with sautéed onions, raw peppers, a pinch of cayenne and salt, sauté for 5 minutes .
5. Garnish with cilantro and a wedge of lime.
Serve with rice and salad.

Black beans have 7-8 grams of protein and 60 mg of calcium per 1/2 cup, help prevent constipation, lowers cholesterol, combats cancer and help to stabilize blood sugar.

Ginger Broiled Salmon

Ingredients:
1 tablespoon coconut oil
1/4 cup water
2 teaspoons fresh grated ginger
1 tablespoon umeboshi plum vinegar
2 4-ounce wild salmon fillets
1 tbsp extra virgin olive oil
1/4 cup chopped onion
2 cloves garlic
Large bunch of red or green Swiss chard

Directions:
1. Make marinade by combining oil, water, ginger and vinegar.
2. Place fish in a shallow baking dish, cover with marinade, and refrigerate for 30 minutes.
3. Preheat broiler.
4. Broil fish skin side down for 6-8 minutes.
5. Baste with remaining marinade once or twice while broiling.
6. Use any remaining marinade as a sauce and serve (see suggestion below).
• Double marinade recipe, sauté 1/2 of mixture in pan until reduced by half to make a reduction to drizzle over fish

Serve with sauteed swiss chard and brown rice from Monday.

Roasted Cauliflower with Fresh Herbs and Parmesan

6 cups of cauliflower florets
1 1/2 Tbsp extra virgin olive oil
3 garlic cloves, minced
1 tsp parsley
1 tsp tarragon
1 tsp. of thyme
1/4 cup of freshly grated parmesan cheese
1 Tbsp of fresh lemon juice
1/2 tsp. of salt
1/4 tsp. black pepper

1.) Preheat oven to 450 degrees.
2.) Place cauliflower in a large roasting pan. Drizzle with oil; toss well to coat.
Bake for 20 minutes or until tender and browned, stirring every 5 minutes.
3.) Sprinkle with parsley, thyme, tarragon, and garlic. Bake 5 minutes.
4.) Combine cauliflower mixture, cheese and remaining ingredients in a large bowl. Toss well to combine.

*Serve with leftover black beans and salad
*Can use leftover cauliflower for soup, or mash as a side dish later in the week.

Cauliflower contains calcium, protein and is high in vitamin K

Brussel Sprouts with Maple Mustard Sauce

2 Tbsp extra virgin olive oil
1/4 cup of minced onion or shallots
4 cups (1 pound) brussel sprouts, halved or quartered
lengthwise (or left whole if tiny)
1/2 tsp Himalayan or sea salt (to taste)
4 to 6 Tbsp of water
1/4 cup Dijon mustard
2 Tbsp pure maple syrup

1. Swirl olive oil in medium size skillet over medium heat.
2. Saute the onion for 3 to 5 minutes, until it begins to soften.
Add the brussel sprouts and salt, and saute for 5 minutes.
3. Sprinkle in 4 tbsp of water, stir the pan, and cover. Cook the
brussel sprouts until bright green and fork-tender, 5 to 8
minutes. If brussel sprouts start to stick, add a little more
water.
4. Whisk mustard and maple syrup together in a small bowl.
Add this mixture to the pan and stir to combine, season with
freshly ground pepper and serve.

These are even good served at room temperature.
*Serve with a lean white meat, fish or tofu and salad

Vegetable Cabbage Soup

2 Tbs. extra virgin olive oil
1 medium onion chopped
2-3 carrots chopped
2-3 celery stalks chopped
1/2 head of cabbage chopped
3 cloves garlic minced
Salt and pepper
1 can whole tomatoes
3 cans water
2 Tbsp vegetable powder
1-2 cups frozen corn
Handful of chopped fresh parsley

1. Sauté onions in olive oil until translucent, add carrots, celery, garlic, cabbage, salt and pepper.
2. Pour off liquid from canned tomatoes into pot and then crush tomatoes by hand and add them into soup. Use can to measure out three cans of water into soup.
3. Add 1/4 cup vegetable powder and simmer till vegetables are soft.
4. Add frozen corn and chopped parsley towards end of cooking time.

Can add any left over vegetables that you have in the fridge. If raw, add in at the beginning; if cooked, add at the end of cook time. This always makes for the best soups; just know you will never recreate it exactly.

Dinner Menu Suggestions – Week Nine

Monday
Homemade Turkey Soup with a salad

Tuesday
Coconut Curry Chicken and Green Beans
Brown Rice

Wednesday
Chick Pea Salad

Thursday
Fragrant Flavored Rice and Salad

Friday
Orange ginger sauce with chicken or fish
Brown rice and a Big salad

Breakfast suggestion

<u>**Ezekiel French Toast**</u>; scrabble two or three eggs in wide bowl, add 2 tbsp water, 1 tsp vanilla, and a shake or two of cinnamon or all spice. Dip bread in letting each piece soak for a few seconds, place on hot skillet, coated with ghee or coconut oil, cook till golden. Serve with real maple syrup on top.
Throw on some berries, feeling ambitious try a fried banana with it, slice down the middle, place in same skillet with a little butter, cook a few minutes till soft, drizzle with maple syrup or honey.

Grocery Shopping List - Week Nine

Ginger root
Organic carrots
Organic celery
Lemons
Organic romaine or mixed greens
Organic tomatoes
Onions
Garlic
Bananas
Jalapeno
Green beans
Basil, Thai if possible
Lemon grass (jar if necessary)
Red bell pepper
Tomatoes
Fresh mint or basil
Oranges

Eggs
Ezekiel bread
Brown Rice
Basmati Rice
Granola
Green tea
Peanut or almond butter
Ghee
Organic brown sugar
Organic butter

Organic milk, rice or almond milk
Feta cheese
Can of Chick Peas or dried

Extra virgin olive oil
Organic coconut oil
Can of coconut milk
Chicken flavoring
Red wine Vinegar
Low sodium soy or tamari
Honey
Cinnamon
Cinnamon sticks
Whole cloves
Cardamom pods
Cumin
Sea salt
Crushed black peppercorns
Turmeric
Saffron
Bay Leaves
Red or green curry paste
Fish sauce
1 lb chicken or 1 pkg extra firm tofu

"Science validates what our grandmothers knew. ...

Stock contains minerals in a form the body can absorb easily—not just calcium but also magnesium, phosphorus, silicon, sulphur and trace minerals. It contains the broken down material from cartilage and tendons-stuff like chondroitin sulphates and glucosamine, now sold as expensive supplements for arthritis and joint pain."
Taken from "Broth is Beautiful" by Sally Fallon
Sally Fallon is a spokeswoman for the Westin Price Foundation, they teach the benefits of raw milk and animal protein.

When I got you started on this program I told you that I was a flexitarian. I have strong feelings about being a healthy vegetarian; however the occasional meat or broth, I personally believe is healthful. We are raising our awareness about what goes into our bodies. Who wants to eat meat from a dead animal that has a lifetime of suffering, been traumatized, filled with fear and then slaughtered? Remember, we are what we eat. It's not just the antibiotics and growth hormones that you need to be concerned with; it's the way the animal has been cared for. If they are filled with fear and anger, then you will be putting that into your body as well. Be aware that factory farming exists.
Now that's, "food for thought."

Homemade Turkey soup

Carcass of organic turkey (use the meat for sandwiches)
2 tbsp olive oil
1 large onion
3-4 stalks celery
4-5 carrots
1 tsp Chicken flavoring
1/2 cup brown rice
2-3 bay leaves

1. Place bones of turkey in a large pot, cover with water, bring to a boil then turn down heat and simmer for 60 minutes or so, turn off heat and let cool. The longer you simmer and steep the bones the more protein in the broth.
2. Strain bones from broth.
3. In separate pan sauté onions in olive oil; add carrots and celery, sauté 2-3 minutes and then add to broth.
4. Pick turkey meat from bones and add back into broth with bay leaves.
5. Turn on medium low heat and cook about 30 minutes, rinse rice and add, (adjust amount of rice to proportion with the amount of broth you have, it swells a lot) and cook another 45 minutes.
Add salt and pepper to taste.

Coconut curry chicken and green beans

1 tbsp extra virgin olive oil
2 cloves garlic minced
Jalapeno deseeded and minced (adjust amount to your liking)
1 can coconut milk
2 tbsp green or red curry paste
1 tbsp brown sugar
1 tbsp fish sauce
3 cups green string beans cut in half, and cooked al dente
2 –3 tbsp fresh basil (use Thai basil if you find it)
1 tbsp fresh minced lemon grass (may use jar version found in the Asian section)
Red bell pepper strips (optional)
1 lb sliced chicken or drained and pressed extra firm tofu
2 cups cooked brown rice

1. Sauté garlic and jalapeno in olive oil for one minute.
2. Add coconut milk, curry paste, brown sugar, lemon grass and fish sauce, and sauté for 3 or 4 minutes.
3. Add chicken or tofu, and continue to cook until cooked through.
4. Add cooked string beans, red bell pepper strips and basil, and remaining coconut milk.
*Serve over rice.

Chick Pea Salad

1 can chickpeas drained and rinsed
2 tomatoes cut into chunks
1/4 to 1/2 brick feta cheese
1/4 cup fresh mint leaves (may substitute basil)
1/3 cup Red wine vinegar (may add more to taste)
1/4 cup Olive oil
1/2 small onion
Sea salt and pepper to taste

*Serve with pita wedges.

Don't get hung up if you don't have an ingredient
Improvise use dried herbs instead of fresh if needed
This makes enough for two fairly large salads
Double recipe if needed

*Chick peas and feta cheese are loaded with protein, onions are an antioxidant/natural cancer fighter and mint is good for digestion. Enjoy!

Fragrant Flavored Rice

1 1/2 cup basmati rice
1 3/4 cup water
2 tablespoons ghee (purified butter)
1 cinnamon stick
5 whole cloves
4-5 crushed cardamom pods
1/2 tsp cumin
1/2 tsp crushed black peppercorns
2 bay leaves
1/4 teaspoon turmeric
1/4 teaspoon salt
6 strands saffron (optional)

1. Wash the rice until water is clear.
2. Heat a large saucepan on medium heat and add the ghee, cinnamon, cloves, cardamom, cumin, peppercorns, and bay leaves. Stir for a moment until fragrant.
3. Add the turmeric and salt to the spices and then the drained rice, sauté for a minute or two.
4. Pour in the water, cover and bring to a boil. Turn down the heat to low and cook, covered for about 15-20 minutes, fluff gently with a fork and serve.

Cooking option: If you would like this recipe to be a full meal you can add in a protein during step 3, such as tofu, chicken or lean meat. When adding to spice mixture, may need a touch of water, cook thoroughly then remove protein from pan, save aside, add rice and water to same pan and cook till done, adding protein back in at end.

Orange Ginger Sauce
(serve over fish, chicken or tofu)

- 1 tbsp virgin coconut oil
- 1 tbsp soy sauce or tamari
- 1 tbsp honey
- 1 tbsp orange zest
- 3 tbsps fresh orange juice
- 1 medium garlic clove, peeled and chopped
- 1 piece fresh ginger root (about 1 inch) peeled and chopped
- 1/4 tsp salt

1. Process all ingredients in food processor or blender, scraping down sides as needed, until smooth.
This can be used with fish, chicken, tofu, or even as a dressing.

Serve with brown rice and a big salad.

This recipe was taken from page 155 of the Virgin Coconut Oil cookbook.

Dinner Menu Suggestions - Week Ten

Monday
Falafel with Dill Dressing, Served with salad

Tuesday
Egg Enchiladas
Ezekiel Toast

Wednesday
Easy Mac and Cheese
Smart Dogs or Beef hotdogs (without nitrates) and Sauerkraut

Thursday
Roasted asparagus with lemon
Wasabi mashed potatoes
Pan fried chicken and Salad

Friday
Orange Halibut
Sautéed greens (your choice) kale is suggested and Salad

Breakfast suggestions

Try adding in a smoothie this week. Keep frozen fruit in your freezer. In a blender add frozen fruit, Kefir (a liquid yogurt/probiotic), protein powder, flax oil, (flax oil, must be stored in refrigerator) banana and agave syrup to taste.

Grocery Shopping List - Week Ten

Bunch of asparagus
Leafy greens
Lemons
Organic romaine or mixed
greens
Organic tomatoes
Onions
Red onion
Garlic
Bananas
Cilantro
Cucumber
Potatoes
Eggs
Ezekiel bread
Whole wheat bread
Brown Rice elbow pasta
Flour (oat or garbanzo)
Brown Rice
Granola
Plain Greek yogurt
Corn tortillas or whole wheat
Monterey Jack cheese
Salsa
1 Can of chick peas (garbanzo
beans)

Can black olives (sliced)

Organic orange marmalade
Sauerkraut (Bubbies is a good
brand)
Condiments, broths, oils
Extra virgin olive oil
Organic coconut oil or
grape seed oil
Wasabi paste
Panko bread crumbs (Japanese)
Cumin
Coriander
Sea salt
Cayenne pepper
Dill
Turmeric
Specialty
Halibut or other white fish
Organic hotdogs (no nitrates)

Falafel with dill dressing

1/4 cup red onion minced
1 can garbanzo beans rinsed and drained
2 garlic cloves
2 slices whole wheat bread
2 tbs. panko/plus more to coat
1 tbs. extra virgin olive oil
1 tsp cumin
1 tsp coriander
1/2 tsp tumeric
1 tbs. fresh cilantro or parsley (or both)
1 egg beaten
Pinch sea salt
Pinch cayenne
2 tbs. organic coconut oil or grape seed oil

1. Place onion, garbanzo beans and garlic in food processor.
2. Transfer to bowl, add bread, panko, spices and egg.
3. Mush together with hands and form 1 1/2 inch balls, roll in panko crumbs and then press into patties.
4. Place in hot skillet with oil and sauté, turning occasionally till golden brown; or patties may be cooked on baking sheet in 375 degree oven for 20 minutes.

Dill dressing

1/2 cup plain Greek yogurt
1/2 cucumber minced fine
1 lemon
1 tsp dill
Pinch sea salt
Mix all ingredients in small bowl and drizzle over falafel.

Egg Enchiladas

6-8 eggs
2 tbsp milk
6-8 corn or flour tortillas
1/2 cup shredded Monterey Jack cheese
Fresh salsa
Sliced black olives (optional)

1. Scramble eggs with milk; add a pinch of sea salt and 1/4 cup of the cheese.
2. Warm tortillas shells over lightly oiled skillet.
3. Fill with egg mixture, a spoonful of salsa and roll up.
4. Place seam side down in baking dish. Cover with remaining cheese, salsa and black olives.
5. Place in 350 degree oven for 10-15 minutes until heated through.
* Serve with Ezekiel toast

To lengthen thy life, lessen thy meals.
~Benjamin Franklin

*Don't overcomplicate it, stay away from junk food,
and chemicals.
Eat mostly veggies and enjoy an occasional treat.

Easy and Healthy Mac & Cheese

1 package brown rice pasta (elbows or other small shape)
1 cup shredded cheese, Monterey Jack or cheddar
1 tsp oat flour (may use other organic flour)
2 tbsp organic milk
2 tbsp organic butter

1. Boil pasta till al dente usually little less than 10 minutes.
2. While pasta is cooking melt butter in a large sauce pan.
3. Whisk in milk, flour and cheese till melted and blended well.
4. Drain pasta and pour into cheese mixture, stirring well to coat.

Roasted Asparagus with Lemon

Roasting brings out the natural sugars in the Asparagus and all of the nutrients stay inside.

1 bunch of Thin Asparagus (thicker ones work well too, but aren't as sweet)
2 tsp Extra Virgin Olive Oil
Sea or Himalayan Salt
2 tsp Fresh Organic Lemon Juice

1. Place rack in center of oven. Preheat oven to 400°F.
2. Wash and drain Asparagus and pat dry. Remove bottom end
of spear by snapping off.
3. Place in large enough baking pan to hold all in single layer tossed with olive oil and sprinkle with salt.
4. Roast 10–15 minutes or until tender (bite into one to check), depending on thickness.
7. Pour lemon juice over asparagus. Taste for salt.

Wasabi Mashed Potatoes

5 or 6 Organic white potatoes
1/4 cup Organic milk
2 Tbsp. Organic butter
1 tsp. Wasabi paste

1. Cut potatoes into large equal chunks, unpeeled. The vitamins are in the skin, but if you don't want to see the skin then buy all means peel them.
2. Boil till fork tender, about 20 mins. and drain well.
3. Add milk a little at a time and butter, use either a potato masher or a beater, add a little wasabi to taste.

*I love to serve this with fish and salad.

Orange Halibut

4–6 fillets of halibut or other white fish (depending on family size)
1/2 cup organic orange marmalade
3 tbsp. orange juice
Black pepper to taste or red pepper flakes (if you like it spicy)
1 tbsp fresh chopped parsley

1. Place fish fillets in bottom of casserole dish.
2. Combine marmalade, orange juice, and pepper, spread over fish and cover. Place in 350 degree oven for 30 minutes or until fish is done. Sprinkle with chopped parsley and serve with brown rice or quinoa, sautéed kale and a salad.

Dinner Menu Suggestions – Week eleven

Monday
Spinach, Beans and Pasta Soup and Served with salad

Tuesday
Pineapple Chicken with Black Bean Sauce
Served with brown rice

Wednesday
Polenta topped with Dandelion Greens
Served with salad

Thursday
Eggplant Parmesan and Salad

Friday
Bay Scallop Stew
Whole grain crackers and Salad

"Eat when calm. If you eat in a stressful environment
your body goes into fight or flight, you are on adrenaline,
which inhibits the processing of nutrients."

Grocery Shopping List - Week Eleven

2 bags spinach
Scallions
Ginger root
2 bunches dandelion greens
2 firm eggplants
Organic carrots
Organic celery
Lemons
Organic romaine or mixed greens
Organic tomatoes
Garlic
Bananas
Eggs
Ezekiel bread
Whole Wheat Bread
Brown rice pasta (shell shape)
Flour (oat or garbanzo)
Brown rice
Granola
Green Tea
Peanut or almond butter
Ghee
Mozzarella Cheese
Organic butter
Organic milk, or almond mild
Parmesan Cheese
Tahini (sesame paste)
Raw almonds

Sesame seeds
Nori sheets
20 oz. can pineapple
Black bean sauce
Corn grits

Whole wheat bread crumbs (easy to make yourself)
3 cans canellini beans or dried
Can of whole organic tomatoes

1 Can of chick peas (garbanzo beans)

Extra virgin olive oil
Large organic chicken broth
Pure maple syrup
Grape seed oil

Cumin
Coriander
Sea salt

1 lb. boneless organic chicken
1/2 lb bay scallops

Spinach, Beans and Pasta Soup

3-5 cloves garlic, minced
2 tbsp olive oil
1 large carton organic chicken broth or homemade
2 bags spinach
3 cans canellini beans
1/4 box pasta shells or other small shape, cooked
Sea salt and black pepper
Parmesan cheese

1. Sauté garlic in olive oil until fragrant, add chicken stock. 2.
2. Drain and rinse canellini beans, place 2 cans in blender or food processor, puree and then add to broth.
3. Add spinach to broth and cook down, add remaining can of beans.
4. Add in al dente cooked pasta, season to taste.
*Serve with grated cheese on top.

On a scale of 1 to 10, you should eat to a 7. Never be too hungry or too full. Your digestive tract is being stressed when you overeat, plus it gets use to the large portions. On the other end of the scale we are hurting ourselves by skipping meals. The body thinks there is a famine going on so it will start to store fat to have ample fuel until the next famine.

88

Pineapple Chicken with Black Bean Sauce

1 tbsp extra virgin olive oil
4 medium scallions, chopped (green and white parts)
1 Tbsp fresh ginger root, chopped
2 medium garlic cloves, minced
1 pound uncooked boneless, skinless organic chicken breast, cut into 1-inch cubes
20 oz canned pineapple, packed in juice, use tidbits
1/4 cup black bean sauce
2 cups cooked brown rice, kept warm

1. Coat a large skillet with olive oil and set pan over medium-high heat.
2. Add scallions, ginger and garlic; cook until soft, about 3 minutes.
3. Add chicken and cook until lightly browned on all sides, stirring often, about 5 minutes.
4. Add pineapple (with its juice) and black bean sauce to skillet; bring to a simmer; until chicken is cooked through, about 5 minutes more.
5. Divide rice among 4 shallow bowls and spoon chicken mixture over top.

*This recipe can be done with fish or tofu, if using tofu remember to drain well before cubing.

Polenta Topped with Dandelion Greens
Adapted from "Greens Glorious Greens!" cookbook

Ingredients
3 1/2 cups water
1 cup corn grits
2 cups water
2 bunches dandelion greens
2 tsp olive oil
2 tsp minced garlic
Salt and pepper to taste
1/3 cup parmesan cheese
Lemon wedges

1. In a large heavy bottomed pot, bring water to a boil.
2. Slowly whisk in corn grits and salt, continuously stir until mixture thickens. Turn heat to low and cook uncovered for 20– 30 minutes, stirring often to prevent sticking.
Polenta is ready when mixture pulls away from sides and a wooden spoon will stand up in the center.
3. Spread polenta into an 8x8 inch pan or a pie plate. Refrigerate uncovered until polenta cools – at least half an hour, until it is firm enough to cut with a knife

4. In a large skillet with a lid, bring 2 cups water to a boil. Add dandelion greens that have been washed, stemmed, chopped, and sprinkled with salt, boil for 3 -4 minutes. 5. Drain and set aside, saving cooking liquid for drinking. (drink this liquid like tea, it is called pot liquor, very good for you and very delicious) 6. Wash and dry skillet, in the same skillet, heat oil over medium heat. Add garlic and sizzle for 30 seconds to 1 minute. 7. Add cooked dandelion greens and salt, stir to coat greens with garlicky oil. Cover and cook for 1 minute, until greens are hot.

8. To grill polenta, brush a cast iron skillet or stove top griddle with olive oil. Cut polenta into 2-3 inch squares and grill for 3-4 minutes on each side, till golden.

9. To serve, place polenta on plates and distribute greens along center of polenta. Sprinkle with cheese and serve with lemon wedges.

*Dandelion greens are rich in fiber, potassium, iron, calcium, magnesium, phosphorus and the B vitamins, thiamine and riboflavin, and are a good source of protein.

Eggplant Parmesan

2 firm eggplants
Extra Virgin olive oil or
grapeseed oil
Sea salt
3–5 eggs
Flour
Whole wheat bread crumbs
Marinara sauce (recipe below)
Parmesan cheese
Mozzarella

1. Slice eggplant into 1/4 inch slices, place on top of paper towel on plate, sprinkle with salt and then place another paper towel on top, layer eggplant sprinkled with salt and topped with paper towel until both eggplants are cut. Place another plate on top with a heavy object on top. This will press the moisture out of the eggplant and cut any bitterness. It will leak water so be careful where you place it, over a cutting board with an indent for drippings works well.

2. Scramble egg with a tbsp of water in one bowl, place flour in another bowl, and bread crumbs in another.

3. Dip eggplant slices first in flour, then egg, then breadcrumbs, fry in oil on medium heat until golden.

4. Transfer eggplant to paper towels to drain.
5. In large casserole dish layer marinara sauce, eggplant, sprinkle with parmesan and a light sprinkle of shredded mozzarella cheese.
6. Continue to layer until all eggplant is in casserole, top with sauce, and add both cheeses. Cover casserole dish.
7. Bake in oven at 350 degrees for approximately 30 minutes or until all cheese is melted and casserole is bubbly. Take cover off for last few minutes if you desire a golden top.
We eat this on toasted rolls with salad. It's even better the next day cold on sandwiches.

Marinara Sauce

1 can crushed tomatoes
3 – 4 garlic cloves minced
2 Tbsp Extra virgin olive oil
1 Tbsp dried parsley
pinch crushed red pepper
1 tsp salt

1. Sauté minced garlic in extra virgin olive oil.
2. Add dried parsley, sea salt, dash red hot pepper flakes if you like it spicy.
3. Add organic crushed tomatoes or diced if you want it chunky; let bubble a minute then turn to low for 15 mins.

Bay Scallop Stew

1/2 pound bay scallops
3 cups organic milk (may use skim milk)
1 tbsp butter
Salt and pepper

1. Cover with just enough water and steam till scallops begin to change color, don't overcook.
2. In another sauce pan, melt butter; add milk and cook till warm. Scoop out scallops with slotted spoon, add to milk, and add hot scallop water to soup mixture, salt and pepper to taste.

This recipe works with oysters or cubed fish as well. Adjust amounts to servings needed.

Try some different textures for your salads

If you love fennel, try this:
Toss sliced fennel with a drizzle of olive oil and juice of lemon, salt and pepper to taste, easy and delicious.

If you love celery, try this:
Toss sliced celery with chopped green olives and pimentos,

Dinner Menu Suggestions - Week Twelve

with olive oil and juice of lemon. No salt needed.**Desserts**
Dark Bark
Bean Brownies

Monday
Soba Soup with Spinach, Served with salad

Tuesday
Potato Leek Soup, Served with salad

Wednesday
Oven Roasted Veggies
Served with salad and Leftover soup

Thursday
Warm Beet Salad, Served with rice

Friday
Sesame Seared Tuna
Leftover brown rice and Salad

Snacks (optional recipes)
Easy hummus
Seaweed crunch

Grocery Shopping List - Week Twelve

1 bunch fresh spinach
Shitake mushrooms
Parsley
Bunch of beets with tops
Scallions
Ginger root
Limes
Potatoes
Leeks
Organic carrots
Organic celery
Lemons
Organic romaine or mixed greens
Organic tomatoes
Garlic
Bananas
Eggs
Ezekiel bread
Whole wheat bread
Brown Rice
Granola
Green tea
Peanut or almond butter
Ghee

Blue, gorgonzola or feta cheese
Organic butter
Organic milk, rice or almond milk
Raw walnuts
Sesame seeds
Cold pressed Peanut oil
Miso paste
Tamari sauce
Extra virgin olive oil
Bragg's liquid Aminos
Vegetable or chicken broth
Mirin
Honey
Cold pressed sesame oil
Wasabi paste
Rice wine vinegar
Bay leaf
Cumin
Thyme
Sea salt
Optional small whole organic chicken
Wild caught tuna steaks
(Ingredients for bonus desserts and snack recipes not on this list, must add if making recipes)

Healthy Desserts

Dark Bark

1 pound good quality chocolate ... 70% cocao
1/2 cup cashews
1/2 cup dried apricots
1/4 cup dried cranberries
1/4 cup candied ginger
sea salt

1. Roast cashews and sprinkle with sea salt.
2. Chop apricots into 1/4 inch pieces and finely chop candied ginger.
3. Combine chopped roasted cashews, apricots, cranberries and ginger.
4. Melt chocolate over simmering water in metal bowl or double boiler.
5. Line a baking sheet, approximately 8 1/2 by 11 inches with parchment paper.
6. Pour melted chocolate onto parchment lined tray and spread evenly. Sprinkle fruit and nut mixture evenly over the top and lightly press into chocolate to adhere.
7. Allow chocolate to set in refrigerator.
8. Break into bite-size pieces.

Bean Brownies

1-1/2 cups carob semisweet chips or dark chocolate, 70% cacoa
2 cans black beans, drained and rinsed
4 eggs
2/3 cup agave nectar or
1-1/4 cup date sugar
1/2 teaspoon baking powder
chopped walnuts (optional)
shredded coconut (optional)

1. Place carob chips in a heat-resistant bowl on top of a boiling pot of water until melted.
2. In blender or food processor, combine beans and eggs.
3. Add sweetener, baking powder and melted chips, process until smooth.
4. Pour batter into an approximately 9-inch nonstick pan.
5. Bake at 350 degrees for 45 minutes.
6. Top with walnuts and coconut if desired.
7. Allow to cool cut and serve.

*For mini cupcakes bake at 350 for approximately 10-12 minutes

These are surprisingly delicious, and nobody will be able to guess that they are made from beans!

Soba Soup with Spinach

2 tbs peanut oil
12 oz. shitake mushrooms (stems removed, thinly sliced)
4 scallions, white and green thinly sliced
1 clove garlic minced
1 tbsp fresh ginger minced
5 cups water
1-3 tbsp miso paste
1 bunch fresh spinach
2 tbsp. fresh lime juice
1 tbsp tamari sauce

1. In large saucepan, heat oil. Add mushrooms, scallion whites, garlic, and ginger. Cook gently until mushrooms are tender, about 5 minutes.
2. Add water; bring to boil. Add soba noodles, reduce to simmer, and cook 5 minutes. Add spinach; cook just until tender, about 1 minute.
3. Add lime juice, and tamari sauce. Add miso a tbsp at a time to taste. This is added at the end to preserve its nutritional benefits.
4. Serve topped with scallion greens.

Potato Leek Soup

3-4 large potatoes
1 tbsp olive oil
2 large leeks
1 garlic clove minced
1 tsp Bragg's Liquid Amino's
Vegetable or chicken flavoring (no msg) to taste
1 bay leaf
1/4 tsp cumin
Dash thyme
Fresh parsley for garnish
• optional - small whole chicken

This recipe can be made with chicken or as a vegetarian potato leek soup.
If using chicken:
1. Place chicken in slow cooker and cover with water. Cook 3-5 hours on high. Take chicken out, let cool, shred meat back into broth in slow cooker.
If not using chicken, begin here:
2. Cut potatoes into large cubes, cover with water or place into chicken broth, add remaining ingredients and cook on high 2-4 more hours.
3. Add vegetable flavoring and salt and pepper at end, to taste.
4. Mash a few times by hand with a potato masher; serve with fresh parsley minced on top.

• This recipe can also be made using a large pot, adjust cooking times. The longer the chicken simmers the more nutritional benefits.

Oven Roasted Veggies

Use any combination of bite-sized pieces of scrubbed and unpeeled veggies, such as eggplant, small red potatoes, yellow or green summer squash, mushrooms, asparagus, any root vegetable, and or onions. Toss with crushed garlic and olive oil. Toss in any spices you like, such as rosemary, oregano, tarragon, and or basil to taste. Spread in a roasting pan in single layer and roast approximately 20-30 minutes at 400 degrees, covered. Uncover and roast another 20 minutes stirring occasionally until veggies are tender, salt and pepper to taste. The longer they roast the sweeter they get.

Warm Beet Salad and Rice

Large bunch of beets with tops
1 tbsp olive oil
1 clove garlic minced
1/2 cup walnuts
Blue cheese, gorgonzola or feta

1. Remove beet greens and save.
2. Peel beets and boil till soft.
3. In separate skillet sauté garlic till fragrant and add chopped beet greens, quickly sauté for about a minute, remove from heat.
4. Toast roughly chopped walnuts in oven on 375 degrees for 5 - 7 minutes.
5. Toss together cooked beets, greens, walnuts and crumbled cheese of your choice. Season with salt and pepper and serve along with brown rice.

Sesame Seared Tuna

1 cup soy sauce
1 Tbsp mirin (Japanese sweet wine)
1 Tbsp honey
2 Tbsp sesame oil
1 Tbsp rice wine vinegar
4- 6 ounce wild caught tuna steaks
1/4 cup sesame seeds
1 Tbsp olive oil
Wasabi paste

1. In a small bowl stir together the soy sauce, mirin and sesame oil. Divide into two equal parts.
2. Stir rice wine vinegar into one part and set aside as a dipping sauce.
3. Spread the sesame seeds on a plate, coat tuna steaks with the remaining soy sauce mixture, then press into the sesame seeds to coat.
4. Heat the olive oil in a cast iron skillet over high heat until very hot. Place steaks in the pan and sear for about 30 seconds on each side.

*Serve with the dipping sauce, wasabi paste, rice and salad

"When you know better, you do better."
~ Maya Angelou
Always be armed with healthy snacks. These two snack recipes are so easy and so good that you will even want to serve them to your guests.

Easy Hummus

1 can chick peas, drained
2 heaping tbsp. sesame tahini
2 tbsp olive oil
1/2 tsp. cumin
1 tsp coriander
1-2 cloves garlic
Juice of 1 lemon
1/2 tsp sea salt

1. Combine all ingredients in the food processor and whip it up! Recipes don't get much easier than this one! Keep plenty of cleaned and cut up carrots and celery on hand.

SEAWEED CRUNCH

1/3 cup olive oil
1/2 cup maple syrup
1 cup of cracked almonds
1 cup sesame seeds
6 sheets of nori (torn into small pieces)

1. Heat oil and syrup—toss in almonds and sesame seeds—add nori and mix well over low heat.
2. Spread mixture on cookie sheet into a thin layer. Bake @ 350 for 10 minutes. When cool, break into pieces. Enjoy!

Because you love yourself and your family, you will pledge to avoid...

Partially hydrogenated oil

Contains high levels of trans fats. Trans fats increase harmful LDL cholesterol and decrease good cholesterol, both of which contribute to heart disease, (found in most processed or commercially baked or packaged foods because they never spoil)

High Fructose Corn Syrup

Converts to fat more than any other sugar. It alters the metabolic rate in a way that favors fat storage. It increases the risk of type 2 diabetes, coronary heart disease, strokes, and cancer.

Artificial Colors & Flavorings

Chemical compounds made mainly from coal-tar derivatives. They have been linked to allergic reactions, asthma, skin rashes, hyperactivity, headaches and fatigue. They are used to give color and flavor back to food lost during processing.

White table Sugar

It triggers a vicious cycle of sugar cravings, increased insulin production, increased appetite, more sugar intake, and more insulin production, until you are in a cycle of cravings, bingeing and crashing all day long. Use gentler sweeteners like; maple syrup, honey, really raw sugar, stevia, and dates.

Artificial sweeteners

(aspartame, saccharin, sucralose, sorbitol, acesulfame-K) commonly used in sugar-free baked goods, chewing gum, gelatin desserts soft drinks and diet foods. They have been linked to headaches, dizziness, hallucinations and cancer.

Now you are off to a good start of experimenting and having fun in the kitchen. Use this cookbook as a guide to master a few healthy recipes and go from there. Don't be afraid to try your own combinations. Just remember we want to eat less meat, think of meat as a condiment. Let the vegetables take up half the plate, 1/4 for your grain, 1/4 for your protein. Vary your food, add fruit, and look for a variety of colors. All fruits and vegetables offer different vitamins and minerals so you want to cover all bases by eating a colorful variety.

Burn the rice, not literally but that may happen too. We never want to get discouraged, If you mess up a recipe try again. I have tried to keep all these recipes fairly simple. With a little practice you will see that the real focus is in eating whole nutritious foods and not in becoming a seasoned chef. Although, you may become inspired and find that hidden desire!

Once you start playing around with real food, your energy increases, you become clearer and you start to reconnect with your inner passion.

Thank you for taking this journey with me and sharing our love for food and life. If you would like more information you can visit www.CookinYogi.com. Please feel free to contact me if you have any questions or comments, you can reach me at Sherri@CookinYogi.com.

Namaste,

Sherri, The Cookin' Yogi